STACEY GREGG

Stacey Gregg's other plays include *I'm Spilling My Heart Out Here*, produced as part of the National Theatre's Connections Festival in 2013; *Lagan* at Ovalhouse, London, in 2011, *Perve* at the Abbey Theatre, Dublin, in 2011 and *When Cows Go Boom,* as part of the Abbey Theatre's 20:Love series of public readings in 2008. Her first play *Ismene* was shortlisted for the Royal Court Young Writers' Festival. She was subsequently on attachment at RADA, and commissioned through Rough Magic's SEEDS programme to develop *Grand Tour*. She is Creative Associate at Watford Palace Theatre. Stacey also writes for screen and is developing an original television series and a one-off drama.

Stacey Gregg

OVERRIDE

NICK HERN BOOKS

London

www.nickhernbooks.co.uk

A Nick Hern Book

Override first published in Great Britain in 2013 as a paperback original by
Nick Hern Books Limited, The Glasshouse, 49a Goldhawk Road, London W12 8QP

Cover image: Mandy Horton
Cover design: Ned Hoste, 2H

Typeset by Nick Hern Books, London
Printed in Great Britain by Mimeo Ltd, Huntingdon, Cambridgeshire PE29 6XX

A CIP catalogue record for this book is available from the British Library

ISBN 978 1 84842 367 1

Override was first performed at Watford Palace Theatre on 2 October 2013, with the following cast:

MARK	Geoffrey Breton
VIOLET	Matti Houghton

Director	Selina Cartmell
Designer	Alex Lowde
Lighting Designer	Colin Grenfell
Sound Designer & Composer	Isobel Waller-Bridge
Video Designer	Duncan McLean

'The promise offered by human enhancement technology is at once exciting and unsettling, bringing into sharp focus both our hopes and fears about the future, while challenging our sense of identity as humans [...] In a society that constantly strives for better, faster and smarter, how much freedom should we have to take advantage of new ways to improve our mental and physical performance?'

Emily Sargent,
Superhuman Exhibition, Wellcome Collection

'Those who live a century or two after us and despise us for leading lives so stupid and tasteless, perhaps they'll find a way to be happy.'

Anton Chekhov, *Uncle Vanya*

'All those moments will be lost in time, like [*coughs*] tears in rain. Time to die.'

Hampton Fancher and David Peoples, *Blade Runner*

Characters

MARK
VIOLET

Author's Note

Dialogue in brackets is most likely unspoken.

When we arrive in the play, the style might feel retro or
bricolage, as though we could be in the 1960s, or 1990s, or an
unplaceble contemporary space. As long as we do not feel we
are seeing something 'futuristic'.

References

Elaine Graham's *Representations of the post/human*, John
MacInnes and Julio Pérez's essay, *The Reproductive Revolution*,
Donna Haraway's *A Cyborg Manifesto*, the Wellcome Trust
Superhuman Exhibition, Jared Lanier's *You are Not a Gadget*,
the art and work of Floris Kaayk, Naomi Mitchison, Patricia
Piccinini, *H+ Magazine*. Thanks to CRASSH, Prof. Sarah
Franklin, Prof. Jenna Ng, Kevin Warwick, Jane Fallowfield,
Deborah Pearson, Chris Gregg, Laura Lomas, Brigid Larmour.

*This text went to press before the end of rehearsals and so may
differ slightly from the play as performed.*

ONE

OVERRIDE

Somewhere rural. It's a sunny day.

A cottage feel. An open fire, unlit.

Birds can be heard outside when it's quiet. Right now, however, bad pop music plays at volume.

Evidence of someone who considers themselves cultured: a classic print on the wall, a small, ornamental collection of serious-looking books.

On the floor are a hanging basket and a window box, laid out on a sheet to catch the soil, though some has scattered, messily. The basket is ready for planting. The box is complete with an assortment of plants. A mucky trowel discarded nearby.

He sits on a couch. She is on her knees, having set aside whatever she was potting.

He is particular. He doesn't slouch. He likes his cutlery clean and his underwear folded. She is slapdash. Sensual. She opens things in shops to smell them, even when they aren't testers. She guestimates ingredients when cooking.

She has just told him something.

MARK	(*Over the music.*) Turn it OFF

The music stops abruptly.

What'd you say?

VI	It's probably a mistake.

She tries to catch his hand.

MARK	DON'T.

She is stung.

I just mean. Your hands are dirty.

She looks at her hands. Wipes them on her clothes.

VI   I was in the garden.

She rises, goes and rinses her hands.

Dries them.

She goes to the window. Looks out.
She opens the window.

MARK   What're you doing?

VI   What? Think someone's *listening*?

There's no one for miles.

MARK   Well that fat guy with the dog, Russell, he's /
always –

VI   Don't go all.

Pause.

Cup of tea?

He looks at her, at a loss.

She goes off.

MARK   (*Mutters.*) O your head's falling off? Cup of tea.
Brilliant. Brilliant.

He massages his brow.

(*Calling off.*) So. What'd it say?

Nothing.

Your mother – (*Rueful, to himself.*) Your mother.

VI   (*Off.*) Yeah?

MARK   didn't secure her ah

She re-emerges with a half-full cafetière.

Stops in the doorway.

VI   Assets.

MARK   Yeah.

VI   No.

She sets down the cafetière.

(Of the coffee.) Still warm.

MARK   Sorry, I just want to.

VI   I know.

She pours her coffee.

MARK   Sort this out.

She nods, sips at her drink.

VI   There was a message.

MARK   Right.

VI   An email. Mum's digital assets were frozen. By that company. You know the one always, the one with that annoying man in the ads

MARK   I know it, the loud-voice man, / the

VI   the shouty man exactly

MARK   Right

VI   so cos I'm next-of-kin she's made her assets available to me. There was a licence.

MARK   No passwords?

VI   *(Shrugs.)* You knew Mum, same password her whole life.

He clucks in disapproval.

She pokes at the potting with her trowel.

Told her. First you never listen to your parents, then they never listen to you. Circle of life. As Elton John would say.

(Sings.) 'Ciiircle of liiiife.'

MARK   Can you leave that?

            She leaves the trowel down.

            So – she used the / same password

VI   (*Nodding.*) Same password for everything.

MARK   (*Rolls his head, despairing.*) Date of birth?

VI   Day and the month. And Pickles.
            Our first dog.
            Jack Russell
            Tiny thing.
            Terrible shitter.
            One time it got into the –

MARK   So who's had access?

VI   Other than me?

MARK   Other than you.

VI   Don't know.

MARK   Great. Goody. So. Practically wide to the world.

VI   Obviously I can – we can find out.

            She picks an invisible speck from her coffee.

            Though.
            Maybe we wouldn't want to draw
            you know

MARK   Listen to / what you're saying!

VI   attention, I know but

MARK   Listen!

VI   Mark, calm down.

            She pours him a cup of coffee.
            He doesn't want it.

            I know this is a bit. Hard for you.

MARK   Pf!

VI	The idea of me having had, you know, anything *done*.
	She tries to hold his look, but he turns away.
MARK	Okay.
VI	Uhm – she didn't have much. Assets. Sorted most of the funeral already. Had her headstone paid for – (*Smiling*.) wanted *Flight of the Valkyries* played, you know
MARK	*Flight / of the Valkyries*
VI	(*Demonstrates*.) bum – ba – dum buum buuum, bum – ba-dum BUUM BUUUUUM
MARK	Okay, okay
VI	Okay – . Hadn't seen her in three years.
	Doesn't feel like it.
	She goes to say more. But looks away. Smoothes down her clothes. *She allows the wave of grief to die down.* *He waits, considerate.*
MARK	I know it's hard.
	She takes a breath.
VI	It's okay.
	No one wants to live for ever. I was ahm.
	Going through. Check there was nothing of you know, importance. Just e-receipts, subscriptions. Membership to BBC online, her Bette Midler collection – anyway there it was. Licence. My name.
	He takes this in.
MARK	Did you know?
	Beat.

VI   How – obviously not. *Obviously*

MARK   I know but

VI   it was years and *years* ago, I must've been a kid. I was a kid.

MARK   But is this the / first you've ever

VI   Didn't ring any bells – and I was thinking – if they sedated me, or

MARK   God

VI   you know how quick those things were – then I – I mustn't have realised, maybe.

MARK   No I don't I *don't* know.

            Beat.

            I feel like, sweetheart, suddenly. I don't know you.

            She sets her cup down. Lays a hand on him.

VI   It could mean anything.

MARK   (*Shrugging off her touch.*) Yes! It COULD.

VI   Alright it's a shock, it's / definitely – but –

            I've read about others who never knew. Who had stuff done when they were kids.

            He processes what she's just said.
            He sets down his coffee.

MARK   You've researched it?

VI   What?

MARK   How would you – 'others'?

VI   Nah.

MARK   What 'others'?

VI   Aw – just some article or something.

MARK   You must've searched.

VI	I didn't.
MARK	It wouldn't come up in your cloud.
VI	Well, maybe it was a link – a link to something else.
MARK	Like what?
	He waits for a response.
VI	My family weren't like yours.
MARK	What?
VI	Just. Compared to what you're from, *well off* – it's easier for / you
MARK	What's it got to do / with *anything*?
VI	black and white, it was more black and white for you, it's not black and white, that's all. It's nice, a nice, lovely quality most of the time – cos it makes you sound – confident – can be kinda. Hot.
MARK	Don't – how is it not / black and white?
VI	You know what I mean, you're from this, academic, fancy – your *sister* –
MARK	What about her?
VI	scary. Successful shoes. That awful dinner? *He knows the one.* Couldn't finish my crème brûlée. And I *love* crème brûlée
MARK	I know.
VI	– if I could mainline it with a drip – I was a bleeding, a bleeding stump by the time your family finished a – gaping wound. (*Mimes a fountain of arterial blood.*)

He nods.

Called me (*Airquotes*.) 'earthy'.

MARK   Earthy.

It's still funny.

Called you worse.

VI   I know.

MARK   Pissed ourselves.

You went mad, I'd never seen you like that, drunk
– in possession of a whisk.

VI   Yeah I liked you for some reason, pft! Like a
flipping magician once you got talking

MARK   You were a force of nature. It was – attractive.

VI   Obviously.

MARK   Obviously. I really fucking fancied you.

VI   I really fancied a fuck with you.

He breaks a big smile.

Just I'm just saying Mark, your lot had a different
attitude.

He is annoyed again.

MARK   Look I wasn't having a go at your mum –

VI   It wasn't their fault. People were sold it –
aspirational – attitudes were different.

MARK   Augmentation.
You mean.

What you're talking about.

She nods.
He puts his hands in his pockets. Purses his lips.
Looks off.

VI   Not want your coffee?

MARK   No thanks.

VI   It's delicious, kind of nutty, roasted –

MARK   Violet.

            VI *sighs*.

VI   Okay – right-right – Mum and a couple of mates –
            she said they'd all gone when they were teenagers.
            (*Shrug*.) Everyone was getting it done. Why not?
            They won a trip on a scratchcard.

MARK   Pf.

VI   Had a. Small procedure.

MARK   What'd they have?

VI   Had this tiny bump, over her eye. (*Gestures,
            recalling*.)

MARK   (*Repulsed*.) God.

VI   One of them hid it, Mum said. All her life.

MARK   Medical, or…?

VI   From her husband even. Zap. Better eyes. Pay
            now, upgrade later.

            Beat.

MARK   Where?

VI   Where'd they get it done?

MARK   Yeah.

VI   (*Shrugs*.) Wherever. Before it was banned,
            obviously.

MARK   Definitely?

VI   Definitely.

MARK   Cos

VI	Not supposed to talk about it now but – don't do the looky-away thing –
MARK	I'm not doing the looky-away thing
VI	You are –
MARK	I'm *thinking* actually –
VI	She had it removed, Mark. Didn't want to be – like those Hollywood celebs – awful nose jobs, tattoos. Regretting it. Like Michael Jackson.

Beat.

MARK	Who's Michael Jackson?
VI	I play him all the time, sweetheart.
MARK	That pop stuff.
VI	I like it. He's the king of pop. And Prince is the / prince.
MARK	– what about *you*?
VI	I think. Ahm. I might've been done when I was a toddler.

He absorbs.

I only ah, glanced at the licence.

Was worried – if I kept it open, might draw attention. Pretty sure it's open-access here.

I had a squint.

I've seen pictures.

Must've been holidays. Dad's in a tacky shirt, flipping – I heart something about boobs – and – and I have a little / lazy eye.

Beat.

Sounds old-fashioned, doesn't it?

MARK   You think

VI   Maybe

MARK   You think she had you done. Cos you had a *lazy eye*?

         He gets up and walks around.
         Scratches his head.

         Ha.

         Suddenly he is in her face. He holds her chin and tilts her head to the light.

         Which?

         She gestures to an eye.

         He inspects.

         He lets her be, moves away again.
         She touches her eye self-consciously.

VI   Can you see it from her point of view?
         (*Involuntary giggle.*) O – 'scuse the pun.

MARK   I'm struggling

VI   You're worse than phobic about this

MARK   You're defending her.

VI   Course not.
         Course not, no way.

         Yes.

         He turns back to face her.

         Yes, actually.

MARK   Oho.

VI   She didn't know any better, how could she?

MARK   Brilliant.

VI   It was like smoking no one knew.

MARK	Brilliant.
VI	Used to say it was good for you! Used to smoke when you were preggers. Probably at one time they were like 'shoot heroin it'll make your hair curly!' They were just going about their business.
	And – I left them and moved away here with you. Middle of Nowheresville.
MARK	For *us* – don't say it like that.
VI	Like what?
MARK	That
VI	I don't mean it in a guilt-trippy way I'm saying – I'm just saying I don't know what I'm saying except – (*Emotional.*) I miss her. And I miss Pickles the shitty dog. That's all.
	Her gaze settles on the drinks cabinet.
MARK	You didn't just – your mum and her mates. Got their eyes lasered.
VI	Yeah.
MARK	She took you, you *think*, to have a lazy eye – what – fixed?
VI	Yeah.
MARK	But you said the licence says you had augmentation.
	That's not the same. There's getting things fixed, for *medical* reasons, and there's getting things *better*. Violet.
	She ignores him.
	Okay sorry, you didn't see your mum. Before she. (died)
	But we both agreed to come out here. I didn't make you.

VI	No, I know – I'm just upset.
	I'm happy here. I'm happy.
MARK	So am I.
	Happy.
VI	Just. Not everyone could do that. Make that decision.
MARK	No.
VI	(*Pointed.*) Not everyone was allowed.
MARK	(*Firmer.*) There has to be restrictions.

His comment annoys her.
Impasse.

She reaches for her knitting.
Inspects it.
It's a baby garment. She sniggers.

VI	Who am I? *Knitting.* Pfff.

She tidies it away.
He watches her.

She goes to the drinks cabinet.
Pours a drink.
Smells it. Enjoys smelling it.

Could murder one of these.

He stands, approaches. She offers it to him.
He takes it off her and sets it aside with a clunk.

MARK	Look. We need to say it out, out loud – cos let's face it you / could be
VI	But I don't think so, Mark.
MARK	(*Exploding.*) but you don't remember – you could've had *anything*! I'm – I'm going crazy here

I love you. I don't mean to be shouty but I was
happy and / suddenly I don't know

VI   (*Calm.*) I know.

MARK   Cos if you are augmented.

VI   don't

MARK   then the baby.

          She moves abruptly, wanders off.

          Dusts a shelf with a distracted finger.

VI   Dad. Ahm. Always got me fudge.

MARK   (*Lost.*) Fudge?

VI   Yep. Ahm. When Mum was – working. Just me
          and him, in the car. He'd say, if you're good we'll
          get fudge. Cos there were tests.

          He looks up.

          Blood tests maybe.

MARK   Right.

VI   For a little implant.

          He is agitated.

MARK   How can I trust you? It was there. You knew.

VI   Stop –

MARK   Stop?

VI   as though

MARK   I have to

VI   attacking me

MARK   (*Raising his voice.*) cos I love you sweetheart

VI   Mark, you're overreacting

MARK   I'm scared – I'm scared – what if this is a lie?
None of this is real? Our lovely life, our decisions,
our baby, our BABY, you – you're a LIAR?

*He kicks one of her plant pots. The noise startles
them both.*

She glares at him.

She boots the plant back.

He looks at her, surprised.

She is ripping up the flower box, pulling it apart.

VI   None of this is 'real', is it? Rubbish synthetic crap
I hate this place it's a coffin! You'd bring a baby
into this? *Little cottage little cottage* CRAP. Smell
these? Nice? Organic? o LOVELY – 'they're as
good as real' you said! Astroturf and Easigrass –

She rips up a plant and holds it to him.

That's a begonia!

She shakes it wrathfully in his face.

Looks like nasturtium.
It's a BEGONIA.
Mixed up the bloody – !
What's the point being here if they can't even get
the artificial flowers right! But you LOVE it here –
rustic chic – It's a frigging BEGONIA you TWAT!

Silence.

*She allows the frustration to drain, the begonia
to fall.*
He turns his back on her.

She composes herself.

Sorry.

*She pats the begonia half-heartedly back into
its box.*

She stoops down, on her knees, using her hands to sweep the mess.

MARK   Disgusting.

              Would you have sex with one?

              She stops.

VI   *No.*

MARK   Live with one?

VI   Mark.

MARK   Talk to it like it was *normal*?

VI   it's *not* the same, course I wouldn't sleep with a Companion.

              And *you're* not sleeping with one, as impressive as I am. Cos a bit of augmentation does not make you a flipping robot, pea-brain.

MARK   Sick. You bring this to me this news, this bloody newsflash and don't expect me to be a bit? I'm a bit upset, actually – cos I'm freaking out you're not the person I – You said you'd never have anything done, the thought of it 'turned your stomach' – you came with me on *protests*, Vi.

VI   I know.

MARK   – all those anti-tech protests

VI   (*Laughing.*) those awful hats you used to wear

MARK   this isn't funny

VI   No you're right – just that awful one you had / though

MARK   Violet you helped me get this place and

VI   So funny

MARK   came out here, to get away from all that

VI	perched on your little head

He goes to her.
Strokes her hair.
She smiles at him.
He grips her hair tight. She gasps.
She pushes him softly away.

He puts space between them.

He makes a gesture: the birdsong stops.

MARK	Might go for a walk.

Pause.

I want to trust you.

I don't think –

She nods.

I couldn't.

I know there are people who're – who'd tolerate,
maybe. Who'd say, might say.
React differently.

But we know better.

VI	I understand.

But. Our family. / Our baby.

MARK	don't
VI	Our baby Mark
MARK	'a' baby
VI	(*Shocked.*) our baby
MARK	'a' baby
VI	Don't, Mark
MARK	'a' baby that might be
VI	it's not

MARK   hybrid.

Fucking.
Anything.
Hybrid.
Born to something with *that* in it.
Tech bits. Machine. Dead stuff.
Creepy.

You're messing with my head, Vi.

VI   Sorry.

MARK   I know.

VI   Sorry.

But. We'd know. / We'd just know if I was like
that

MARK   (*Shouting.*) You WOULDN'T. How do we find
out without – we need to get you scanned so I
know what you are, I'm not with a.

You'll be done for Contempt of Flesh.

They could profile you any second.

VI   Trust me.

MARK   I can't.

I *did*, but.

Okay it's not your fault, you were a kid – but. It's
disease, messes with your unborn child. What
mother augments their child?

VI   (*Bursting.*) Thousands! Millions who were sold it
– the best biomedical care!

MARK   Don't

VI   The *best* cosmetics – she was just doing the same
as everyone else. Would you stand back while
other people's kids got better chances?

He is shaking his head.

You *could* understand. But you – you only ever access things you already think – just a big bloody echo chamber here. We need a great big puke.

MARK   O, and what do you do?

VI   I'm still *curious*. I still want to know what other people *think*, *feel*.

She stews.

When was the last time you looked at one of your precious books?

MARK *looks dismissive.*

She goes over, picks one up.

(*Feeling the book.*) Sweetheart. These aren't pumped full of sponsorship – take me places I'd never see in the cloud. I know – I know I sound stupid
but –

It wasn't always like this and it wasn't that long ago. And I think, I reckon in the future it'll change again, and people'll laugh at us for being daft.

We're just a splat of neurons Mark, we're not special. People make mistakes, die. We're juice and carbon.

She holds a book up to her ear.

What's that?

Pretends to listen.

The books agree.

MARK   Fanflippingtastic.

She replaces the book.

VI   The *people* here – ugh *little cottage* balls. It's an ILLUSION. You can't get away from technology.

MARK	Of course – *external* stuff – but you can stop putting it *in* you! Why's that funny? Why's that funny?
VI	You're like a vegetarian in leather shoes.
MARK	No I'm not
VI	You ARE you made the protests about Companions, whipped up fear so they'd ban *all* enhancement.
MARK	'No hard tech in a soft body'
VI	Getting your teeth straightened, glasses, vaccines – we've always enhanced –
MARK	for medical necessity
VI	Yes
MARK	not to pimp ourselves up.
VI	Sweetheart, it's *not the same* as Companions!
MARK	Not mutually exclusive.
VI	You're obsessed!
MARK	Enough work done and you're halfway to being a sex bot.
VI	Don't – (*Involuntary laugh.*) Okay – Here's a human: hello. I'm a human, but I have a hole in my heart, duff kidney whatever, so I'm gonna get a bit of tech implanted and I'll be tickety-boo. Hello. HELLO.
MARK	Hi.
VI	Yes, I'm human. Yes? Jazzed up a bit.
MARK	That's not –
VI	Humour me.

MARK   Okay.

VI   Now, 'Hello. I'm a Companion: I am a lump of tech. I'm a flipping glorified toaster. Obviously. I'm the poor man's R2D2. I keep lonely men company.' Right? An enhanced human is still *human*, NOTHING LIKE a machine.

MARK   People got attached. Screwed those *things*. Gave them –

VI   Names? I gave my vibrator a name

MARK   made them –

VI   Mark –

MARK   there was a campaign for Companion marriage!

VI   Mark. That was a tiny percentage of nuts. There are more people who identify as wizards than people wanting to marry a Companion.

MARK   You gave your vibrator a name?

VI   Harold.

MARK   What the fuck?

VI   Companions – always divided people – anyway they've been around for ever – what's a blow-up doll I mean it's just a Companion without a motherboard. Each to their own – there's a long and rich history of men banging inert things so don't be so uptight.

          Pause.

MARK   It's against everything we –

VI   I know.

          And I'm *sorry* – putting us through this.

          Pause.

Just. No matter how much I've had done, I'm not
that.

Pause.

Might've been okay, except.
Now I don't know who's seen the licence. The
extent of it.

MARK   (*Icy.*) You said. It was nothing.

VI   Absolutely. Yes.
                No. If I'm being honest.

MARK*'s eyes have gone very round.*

MARK   Please – do – be honest.

He holds her hand. Hard. Afraid.

VI   You know Mum was on a stick, when I was little?

MARK   (*Controlled.*) mmhm?

VI   Yeah. Then it went away. (*Does a magic gesture.*)

                Pacemaker too. Then the works. Just a plastic
                pump for a heart, Mark.
                Yep.
                Had her eyes lasered.
                Cochlear implant.
                Dentures.
                Prosthesis, the last few years God bless her, a
                beautiful bionic leg.
                Lovely new hips.
                A white. Shiny. Plastic. Pump for a heart.
                Yep.
                Truckloads of drugs. Statins, Warfarin you name
                it, she munched it.
                Therapeutic to a point, but think she got carried
                away. Got the bug. Got the other leg done, Christ
                she was like the Bionic Woman running for the bus.
                Always after the latest gizmo – and you wonder
                why I never said 'pop round Mark, meet my ma.'
                She made a killer raspberry sponge.

MARK   (*Incredulous, queasy.*) Horrible.

VI   Worried she'd ZAP you with her super-eyes?

MARK   SHE DIDN'T HAVE AN ACTUAL HEART –

VI   NO you shut up / for once

MARK   – how much was left of her?

VI   She was a pioneer – medicine can only do what it does now cos of people like Mum. We *needed* disabilities, war vets – to advance the technology. Now people with disabilities don't exist. Mum wouldn't exist. If we haven't 'fixed' them then we just take them out of the equation before they're born; pick another gene –

MARK   Look I agree we shouldn't 'pick another gene'

VI   Good!

MARK   that's exactly why *we're* having a Natural Birth. *No* selection.

   VI*'s hand strays to her belly.*
   A breath.

   They had to – . Look.
   Look.

   People expected total choice –
   You're talking eugenics.

VI   Exactly

MARK   If we allow – Vi – people – your mum – expected *choice* beyond – Would you deselect *our* baby? You can't augment every inch of your body and then deselect your baby cos it's not super enough

VI   nnngGG I KNOW – I can think for myself, I know it's a shock but I can.

MARK   That's creating – a a super a superior class of, that's

   that's a holocaust of *normal* people, Violet.

VI   Maybe you're not 'normal';

            you're just *common*.

            BORING Marky Mark.

MARK   Whoa

VI   Your parents made their money selling tech to
            people like us – and now you separate yourselves?
            – as though we're inferior, as though we're not
            'normal'? A subclass?

MARK   That's why we were radical! Why we're here now!
            Why it had to be a total ban! I know I know it's
            confusing but
            Honey –
            Normal people –
            Consumers –
            You could buy and sell anything to the point of…

            He is closer to her, impassioned.

            People were, they were losing all sense of – *opting
            for* limb augmentation.
            Amputation.
            People were *getting* amputations –
            Cos (*Searching.*) they *could*. Madness. Total –
            over totally fine, undamaged organs, limbs.
            Fashion!
            And the *money* in it! Christ.
            Live longer run faster plug in and the slogans
            'more natural than nature' what the hell? There
            was nothing left of some of them – people
            disappeared they were just walking tech!

            We're on the same side.
            And I hate to say it

VI   Then don't

MARK   I know how it sounds but. The disabled were part
            of that progress – towards their own erasure.

She lunges at him.
Misses.

Goes again. But he holds her fists.
She lets him.
He comes closer.
Inhales her scent. Grounds himself.

You've told me everything?

She looks into his eyes.
She looks away. Nods.

Okay.

He finds her face with his eyes.

Scared me.

Thought – thought you were telling me you're –
not completely – completely –

He buries his head in her.
But above him, she is angry.

Eventually, she gives in.
He sinks into her, a sigh, feels her there.
She holds him.

VI   (*With difficulty.*) It's okay.

She cradles him.
Strokes his hair.

Some moments.

It's okay, Marky Mark.

She gestures: a pop song from the nineties plays at
a low level.

MARK   Must you?

VI   Soothing.

Beat.

MARK   We're supposed to be evolving as a species.

VI   Just give me this.

                She is petting him, humming, bopping along.
                He rubs his eyes.

                Tired?

MARK   (*Soft*.) mmhm.

VI   Not sleeping?

MARK   You know.

                Pause.

                Nightmares.

VI   Mhm.

                She nods, continues stroking him.

MARK   I'm in a building, looking.

VI   O yeah, that one.

                He breathes.

MARK   Go into the foyer or.

                just a dream, had it when I was little, only ahm –

VI   Mhm.

                Pause.

MARK   Never tell you the next part –

                But you've told me everything so…

                Despite himself. He needs to tell her.

                it turns and it's – not you, but.

                I know it won't matter nobody'll know if I just.
                Let it.

                Nobody in the building. Comes ahm close and – I
                let it – ahm and I'm.

                It touches me. It's touching… turns me round
                and… – *sick* but – ah I. I'm breathing and then its
                breathing its weight on me tastes weird and it's my

head's light – worry maybe people can see but I
can't *stop* – just me and this thing, pushing,
behind, inside... – straining, I know it's a – one of
those – but it's just shagging me, so hard I could
cum and I... wake up.
Hard.
You know?
Just a dream.
Right?
Ahm.

*Her hand has drifted towards his lap. She feels
for him.*
He pushes her away.
She snorts. He looks up at her, helpless.

VI   Know what's creepy?
            You.
            You *want* to *screw* one
            A big hard robo-cock

MARK   VIOLET!

VI   build these perfect worlds in your head – but in
            your gut.

            You're a little fascist sometimes, Mark.

            She stands, untangling herself from him.

MARK   Vi

            She goes to the kitchen.

            Violet?

            He watches.
            *She picks up a toaster. It has features that kind of
            make it look like it has a face.*

            She returns with it.

            She brings it, up close to his face.
            He eyes her, uncertain.

VI   Kiss it.

MARK   What?

VI   Kiss it.
Kiss the toaster.
Tongue it.
Finger its little wires.
Look at its little face.

MARK   Stop being

VI   How do you know it doesn't love you?

MARK   (*Cold.*) Toaster doesn't have feelings.

VI   Rude, could say the same about you.

MARK   What – ? I'd hardly – with a toaster.

She drops the toaster.
Begins to walk away.

                (*Spiteful.*) I could override your enhancements.

She looks up, sharply.

VI   (*Uncertain.*) What?

They hold each other's look.

Some moments.

MARK   No one needs to know.

She stares, hard.

VI   What do you mean?

MARK   I might have the coding – ahm – so – any internal ops would just stop

VI   (*Careful.*) You can override my circuits?

MARK   Probably.

VI   Probably?

MARK   Yes.

Long beat.

VI   (*Unnerved.*) How? Mark.

MARK	We'd just have to do it off the grid. / Illegally
VI	How – . Why would you – why do you have that here?
MARK	It was part of screening – when we moved here – security – supposed to sign it back in but –

He stops, making sense of something new.

You didn't get screened.

VI	(*Nodding.*)

He takes it in.

(*Involuntary laughter.*) Can't tell you I was so bloody relieved.

MARK	No.
VI	Everything in boxes and you fannying round with the security doing all the admin cos you think I wouldn't understand and I am I can / tell you now –
MARK	(No – Violet this is serious)
VI	– I am having a party in my head. Thinking well, what he doesn't know won't hurt. Then the screening was brought up, thought that was it. Game over Violet. You'd see it all then. Everything in me.

Couldn't believe my luck.

She holds up her arm.

Twists it in a way that no human arm could twist.

Nanotech! Woooh!

She spins the arm and the room's smart surfaces spin like a kaleidoscope.

Direct interface! (*To the tune of 'Dem Bones'.*) 'M'wires are connected to the motor cortex and the / motor cortex – '

He launches towards her, terrified, and grabs
her still.
The room is as it was.

MARK   (*flipping out*) STOP IT STOP IT

VI   'connected to electrodes – '

MARK   WHAT IS THAT? Let me Override it.

VI   No

MARK   What're you afraid of?

VI   – you!

MARK   What?

VI   I need to think.

MARK   If you love me –

VI   I do.

MARK   Is any of it life-sustaining?

Silence.

Is. Any of it life-sustaining? (*With difficulty.*) Are
you dependent?

Have you had anything done – are you running
anything internally right now that you cannot
live without?

VI   (*Lying.*) No.

MARK   Our hygiene. Our baby's *health*.

VI   But

MARK   Please.
It'll go away.
It'll just shut down, it'll never show up on the
screenings, we'll never have to talk about it again.

VI   I can live with it. I have done.

MARK   I can't, Violet.

Pause.

VI	We were fine. I'm the same person you've loved
MARK	But I know now.

Beat.

All it'll do is stop anything operating. Can dig out any hard tech later.

She flinches.

MARK *chooses not to see* VI's *fear, swept up in his plan, staring at her arm.*

The arm – we'll deal with.

VI	I'll only have one arm.
MARK	In the big scheme…

Beat.

VI	Wanker.

Beat.

MARK	You *amputated* it
VI	I *upgraded* it.

Beat.

It's gorgeous here.
Despite the begonia issue.

I'm knitting booties.
Think bots would knit their babies booties? Do androids dream of lasagne?

MARK	(*Fighting.*) Look. We're happy
	We're alright.
VI	We're okay.
MARK	We're okay. And I want us to be okay – stay like this.
VI	Till – what, for ever?

MARK   Till we die here. Yes. Together.

She nods.

I can't lose you, I'd, I'd fall apart.
No one'll know, we'll get rid of the licence,
somehow, and, and we'll be perfect again.

VI   'Perfect.'

He cups her face.
But he can't kiss her.
She looks sad.

You could be kissing a toaster.
Would it matter? If it told you it loved you?

They stare at one another.

Who are you to say it doesn't?

She goes.

He waits till she has gone.

He stamps on her plants.

He twists his engagement ring.

He gestures impulsively.

MARK   (*A command.*) Override.

A small flash.

VOICE   'OVERRIDE COMPLETE'

He lets out his breath.

She is in the doorway. She stares hard at him,
shocked.

She passes her hand in front of her eye, testing.
She notices the fingers of the hand don't move.
She tries to move them.
Nothing.

He smiles a little, encouraging. They exchange a
long look.

VI   Did you just...?

            He nods.

            But. I didn't give permission.

MARK   I'm the Administrator.

            *She puts her hand across her eyes for some
            moments.*

            *Eventually, she goes to him, as someone
            ghostwalking.*
            He smiles a bit more.
            They hug.

            I'm looking in your eyes, see?

            She slides down on the floor beside him.
            She rests her head on his knee
            She strokes her belly.

            Night.
            He is happy, relieved.
            He gestures. The birdsong resumes.
            He gestures. Cicadas.

VI   I lied to you.

MARK   (*Forced light.*) More? Can it wait till morning?

VI   Didn't need to read the licence.

            Pretty much knew what was in there.

            He is afraid. He hugs her closer.

MARK   (*Soft.*) Can you just. Tell me in the morning,
            sweetheart?

42

TWO

TECHGNOSIS

Night. Some weeks later.

The flower box is set out, the hanging basket up. It looks cosy, perfect. Classical music plays softly.

The door flies open. Lights automatically go on. She is staggering through the door. She is sweating, white. She sinks into a heap.

MARK *arrives at the bottom of the stairs, in pyjama shorts. He rushes to her. Down on his knees.*

MARK   What is it? Hey

            She moans.
            He helps her up.

            He supports her the short distance to a couch. Lays her down.

            He gestures to silence the music.

    (*Frightened.*) Where've you been, sweetheart?

            He rushes to the sink.
            Fills a glass of water.
            Snatches up a clean cloth.

            He returns.
            He sets down the water.
            Uses it to damp the cloth.

    Hey.

            He goes to cool her forehead, but notices blood. He touches it. Horror.

    No.

            Long pause.

She pulls out a red baby booty.
She wears it on her fingers like a finger puppet.
The puppet looks at her then at him.

VI   (*Puppet.*) 'Natural Birth', right?

Disbelief. He covers his face.

She lets the booty fall.

He rubs his eyes.

She smiles at him, seeking affirmation.

MARK   O

She moans.
He finds, and holds her hand.
She breathes in and out. She is not lucid.

VI   Proud?

MARK   I don't understand.

VI   You were right.

MARK   No, you need – medics, you
          you've miscarried, sweetheart

VI   sorry
          sorry

MARK   Sshh

          Shh

He strokes her hand.

She quietens down.

*

The living room. Weeks have passed. He is
dishevelled, lived in. He is reading a book.
Trying to. But restless.

He swipes the page out of habit.
Realises his mistake.
Turns the page properly.

She enters, in a housecoat.
She looks unwell.
One arm is degraded. It is a bionic arm. The
mechanics are showing. The synthetic flesh has
deteriorated.

She stands, smoking a roll-up cigarette in the
doorway, watching him.

MARK   (*Defensive*.) What?

VI   Nothing.

She exhales, raised eyebrows.

(*Polite*.) Don't let me interrupt.

MARK   No I was.

Uh…

VI   Go on.

He shuffles.

MARK   Well I can't with you watching.

He closes the book.

VI   You look hilarious. Little face all – (*Screwing up
her face in mock concentration.*)

MARK   Would you want to live for ever? If you could?

She chooses not to answer.
Takes a long luxurious drag.

Well *you* look ridiculous.

VI   I can put it out, what's your excuse?

He smiles. She puts out the cigarette.

Took me ages to roll that.

She crosses and sits, expectant.

Rub my shoulder? Aches.
Come on.

MARK	O
	but
	He fiddles with the book.
	Should probably ahm.
	…ah
VI	Get over it!
MARK	I don't like touching it!
VI	Tough!
MARK	It's weird!
VI	You're weird!
MARK	It's not enough I have to look at it?
VI	So rude. I'm sore.
	She gestures for him to come over. *He does.*
	He finds a position behind her that is comfortable.
	What're you reading?
MARK	Nothing.
VI	Is it good?
MARK	It's about ah, coping with loss.
VI	O.
	She puts her head to one side, tired. Closes *her eyes.*
MARK	How're you feeling?
	He starts on her good shoulder.
VI	(*Relief.*) O that's good.
MARK	You… okay?
VI	I'm degrading, Mark, so. Not tip-top.

MARK   … Are you keeping your log?

VI   Mmmnyes.

           She watches him out the corner of an eye.

MARK   Hm. That's funny.

           Cos I checked, and none of this week's symptoms
           were filled out. And then suddenly – they were all
           filled out.

VI   O.

MARK   Vi, if you don't fill it out properly I can't help you.

VI   Uff it's so boring.

           He sighs.

           Want to tell me what's up?

MARK   Apart from *this*? (*Her arm.*)

           *He rubs her shoulder, moving gingerly round to
           the bionic arm.*
           He works at a muscle knot.

           A chunk of her skin comes off in his hand.
           He stares at it.

           Ew.

           Ew.

VI   Man up.

           *He discards it, down the back of the chair or
           somewhere. She's oblivious.*

MARK   Can't believe it degenerated so quickly.

VI   What'd you expect?

           Another bit comes off.

MARK   Eugh! Thought prosthetic skin's supposed to be
           longer lasting?

VI	Livingtech™. Once you pull the plug – starts to die.

A moment, like he might retort, but gets on with massaging instead.

Thank you.

He works at it, reluctant to get stuck in at first. But settling down to the task, like easing into a hot bath.

I'm worried about you.

MARK	No I'm the one worrying about *you*.
VI	Well I'm worried about *you*, sweetpea.
MARK	Well no need. (*Brisk.*) Got up this morning, bright and breezy, went for a jog, you know. Along the ferns. Usual route. Said hello to a few people down on the towpath. Russell was out, with his dog, little Cracker, the shitzu cross – bit nosy Russell. Just said you were away – on a trip... – had a shower, smoothie. All before you were up. Read for a bit. I'm getting good at it, reading. Read for a bit cos I couldn't really – that's why I went for a run, actually – hadn't slept much. Can't think straight really, just this. Gaping cavern. Of massive. Sadness... I...

Think I'm
A bit (*Pulls a face.*)

VI	Constipated.
MARK	depressed. That was a depressed face.
VI	Good.
MARK	Having a.
VI	Good. Think it's good for you. Normal. Think it's okay.
MARK	Mm.

VI   As long as you're not.
            I mean.

            I mean
            You wouldn't really *do* it
            would you?
            Something stupid. Wouldn't leave me…

            He pecks the top of her head.

            *She is working at the limb herself now, irritated
            by it.*

            Silly.

            We're just a splat of neurons. Biological
            machines. Well. I always found that reassuring.

            If *you* started talking about (*Limp*.) 'souls' and
            stuff I don't know, coming from you

            It'd weird me out.

            But I get the question: you want to live for ever.

            He stops massaging.

MARK   I don't. I did, maybe. Once.

            It's more you.

            I want you to live.

            She doesn't respond.
            She takes over the massaging.

VI   So – irritating.

MARK   Don't.

VI   Let me

MARK   Don't

VI   I've got it.

MARK   Don't you'll –

VI   I've got it.

MARK   You're breaking the – the

VI   It's my body.

Eventually, she just takes off the limb, completely, with a click and a sigh of relief. It comes apart easily, slots out, clean.

She studies it for a second, held in her other hand like that.

Then lays it down.
Relaxes.
He watches, incredulous, smouldering.
Gags.
Composes himself.

MARK   You enjoyed that.

VI   Don't be daft.

MARK   You did. You're a torture. You're flamboyant.

She doesn't respond.
He shifts around so that he is close beside her.

Honey.

VI   What?

Beat.

MARK   I'm so sorry.

VI   Don't.

MARK   No I'm so sorry.

I'm really sorry.

VI   Don't, baby. Please. It was no one's fault.

He cuddles up to her.

He nudges the discarded limb with his foot.

Oi.

She bats him away, playful.
He gives her space.

She picks up her knitting with her remaining hand.
Remembers. Tuts, glancing balefully at her
discarded limb.
Abandons the knitting.

MARK   Had a long chat with Dad, there, Monday.

IV   O? Send my love?

MARK   I did.

VI   Ask how I was?

MARK   He did.

VI   Did you tell him?

         Silence.

MARK   I will, I just

VI   I know, I know.

MARK   Talked about a few things.

         He's padding around, restless.

         How they're getting on. The weather. They got a
         zebra finch.

VI   A zebra finch?

MARK   A pet. Alison.

VI   Who?

MARK   The finch.

VI   They called it Alison?

MARK   yeah.

VI   Why didn't they get a dog?

MARK   They got a bird!

VI   O!

MARK   Think he could hear something wrong, in my
         voice – . You know how they – it's a parent's job,

right? Like you always say. I was gearing up to
tell him but
Got on to my sister

VI   Yippee.

MARK   – how she's doing, the babies.

VI   (*Hurt.*) Bit insensitive.

Her hand strays to her belly.

MARK   No, not – more, trying to encourage us, but –
saying something sideways.

Sorry.

He kisses her.
They separate.

VI   But you told them I'm feeling better. I'm *fine*.
Not to worry. Right?

He doesn't respond.

What do you fancy for / dinner?

MARK   He said Mum was. They understand how hard it is
for us cos – How wonderful it was I came along.
They're so proud, cos *they* never thought they
were going to have kids and then they had two.

She shifts.

VI   Your dad said that?

MARK   Yeah.

Just. Dropped it into something completely
unrelated.
Trying to remember someone's hairdo. From a
home movie.
Mum's hair, long or short.
They have a real knack for that. 'Does my bum
look big I slept with the neighbour.' 'Pass the
potato I'm a mass murderer.'

Some moments.

VI	Never thought they were going to have kids?
MARK	Apparently not.
VI	O.
MARK	Mum had problems.
VI	…
MARK	They had treatment.

A long moment.

VI	Well.
MARK	Yeah.

Beat.

VI	Cup of tea?
MARK	Say it. Say you told me so.
VI	I don't want to. I don't think that.
MARK	Say it.
VI	No.
MARK	I was selected.
VI	I know.
MARK	I was selected. In a lab. And they never thought to tell me.
VI	They knew how you felt.
MARK	But how could they –
VI	Protecting you.

MARK *twitches.*

MARK	Say it. I can see you're thinking something.
VI	just. Deep down. You knew.
MARK	Never.

VI	Freudian, kind of.
MARK	I don't like Freud.
VI	No but. You hated something. You hate something.
MARK	And I'm it.
	He is beside himself.
	And I punished you.
VI	No you didn't
MARK	I did
VI	You didn't mean – you followed the law.
MARK	fuck it fuck the fucking FUCKING
VI	– (*Helpful.*) fuckity fuck?
MARK	Don't joke I *did this* to you.
	You started dying
VI	(*Correcting him.*) degrading
MARK	*dying*, the minute I ran the Override.
	I k-kil
	I k–
	Is that why you lost.
	Is that why
	(*With difficulty.*) The baby
VI	No.

That was.

No.

Hard pause.

(*Carefully.*) I lost the baby because we didn't want medical tech. No hospital, no drugs. (*Husky.*) It was natural.

MARK *stoops down and shakes hands with her bionic limb.*

MARK   'Thank you Mark thank you!'

VI   What your parents did was just tinkering. Relatively.

MARK   Tinkering!

VI   Like sending you to private school, it's nothing.

MARK   *No*, they wanted a certain –

VI   They'd've told you if you were IVF. Whatever / it was.

MARK   Ah! Baby shopping! Say it ALL, don't abbreviate, sounds so good! (*Cups his hands like a loudhailer.*) Pre-implantation! Genetic! Diagnosis! Embryo profiling! Like a fluffy baby animal in your mouth. Harmless. Lovely. Pipettes and tech YEY I'm a lab baby

VI   (*Shrug.*) No one's pure.

    Silence.

MARK   (*Soft.*) Wish things were simple.

VI   Don't big it up. We're okay. I'll be okay. For a bit longer.

MARK   Bit – Bit longer? *You're dying.* And it's my –

    She stares at him.

    He looks away.

VI   yeah.

    Love you.

MARK   Love you so much.

    I
    (*Choked.*) I ran the / Override.

VI   (*Sharp.*) Get it into your coconut, I would've been
            found out sooner or later.

MARK   How're you still here?

VI   I really don't know.

            Don't know how much of me is what.
            Riddled with it.
            Guessing it's kidney-related. Would make sense.
            Dad's side.
            Something's failing now, anyway.
            Or. Could be a heart problem. What Mum had.
            It was all done before I was old enough to…
            know. So.

            Apart from the arm.
            That was teenage whimsy.
            The Superarm250™ – God, everyone was mad for
            them.
            Yeah, the arm was my fault. Cringe.
            Mum got my dicky eye done, but the tech wasn't
            really there, twenty-twenty vision, nothing super.
            So, I was fourteen, had it refitted with an implant.
            Those specs I wore at college were just fashion by
            the way, I had Super-vision by then: (*Advert
            voice.*) 'See like a hawk.' First time I spotted you
            you were four streets away, eating a Walnut Whip.
            Then it all went haywire, the law changed…
            Easier to just hide it.

            You weren't to know.

            I did tell you a small mountain of lies.

            Let you carry the shopping. Every time. What a
            bitch, huh? Coulda done it with my little finger.
            Poor Marky Mark.

MARK   Don't care any more. I was wrong. I was wrong I
            just want this. You, working, whatever that means.

VI   What, even if I'm a clever programme?

MARK   Don't joke.

VI   Toaster with a face?

MARK   Yes.
Yes.
I think, I think – you're just beautiful.

(*Desperate*.) We could go to someone.

She looks up.

Someone could ah, 'sort us out'.
You're degrading / so fast. I'm scared.

VI   Sure? Cos you felt clean – look at me – but you'd
upload your mind at the drop of a hat. Wouldn't
you? Stick your mind in the cloud and wait to be
immortal. What a load of balls. 'Clean.' The way
you talk about hygiene, might as well be 'god'.
You're the backwards one.

I can only tell you how I *feel*.

I love you.
You love me.

I know you're struggling cos you know you
shouldn't. Shouldn't love me if I have even a grain
of tech in me but you do. Ask your gut cos it's
louder than your head isn't it?
Tell me that's not true.

Tell me how it *feels*.
Tell / me how it *feels*.

MARK   (*Tumbling out*.) Boiling. Urgent. Want to grab –
pull your eyes out – sorry that's a bit –

VI   (*Encouraging*.) Okay –

MARK   I'm telling you what's in my – what I *feel* – I
want to – get you out of my head my heart so
it's clear again but I want to kiss, just ahm lie
with you, forget everything (*Broken*.) I want to

have another baby   and lie in the sun get fat
walk round with my willy out my belly out and
laugh cos it's funny –

VI   (*Smiling.*) Poetry!

MARK   Shuttup I'm trying

VI   No it's good, I appreciate it

MARK   And

VI   and what?

MARK   Just. You're. Perfect.

          Usually hate all that stuff.

VI   (*Fondly.*) You're an idiot.

MARK   Vi, my heart hurts. For you.

VI   Thought we were coming to some kind of oasis,
          paradise. But nothing feels

          She glances out the window.

          Real.

          She turns back to him.

          I'm not perfect, I'm a bit shit. I'm really a bit shit
          actually.

MARK   I wasn't right.

VI   Me neither.

MARK   Could we go somewhere?

VI   (*Hopeful.*) Where?

MARK   Leave here?

VI   Where though?

MARK   Somewhere else.

VI   We couldn't come back, Mark.

MARK   So? I'd rather try.

VI	(*Growing hope.*) You'd do that?
MARK	Yes!
VI	You'd leave?
MARK	Yeah.
VI	Really?
MARK	Maybe.
	Beat.
VI	'Maybe.'
MARK	Yeah maybe.
VI	Okay.
	Beat.
MARK	Think so.

She watches him.
He doesn't look so sure. He's struggling. O, he wishes he could.

Yeah. Maybe. Soon.

(*Small.*) everything's changed so quickly...

VI   Okay.

She lets the hope drain away. It's too much for him.

It's okay, sweetheart. Come here.

He comes to her.

Sh. Okay.

She puts her arm around him. Pets him.

MARK	Sorry.
VI	Sh sh sh.
MARK	We got it wrong.

VI	Don't worry.
MARK	but he died.
VI	I know.
MARK	Our little man.

They hold each other.
She kisses his head.
Soothes him. Hums to him. Some incongruous
nineties tune.

*

MARK	Want your music on?
VI	Nah.
MARK	Come on.
VI	Really? Aw... You're nicer when you're wracked with guilt.

He gestures. Her music plays.

After a moment she begins to dance.

MARK	What're you doing?
VI	Robot dance.
MARK	What?

MARK *is annoyed.*

She laughs.

VI	Looked it up on Mum's BBC archive. It was really popular in clubs and stuff. Back in the day. Am I good?
MARK	That's not funny.
VI	It is a bit funny.
MARK	It's sick.
VI	Sick things are the funniest.

Eventually, he cracks up too, laughing despite himself.

She turns from him, hiding that she is crying.

*

VI *is just a cube-like hub with a voice transmitter.*

Her bionic, non-degrading components, wires and internal hardware are still connected, laid out how they would've been if still her body. Her housecoat is laid out too.

He is much more lived in than before, messy.

The books are in disarray. He has been reading to VI. *He is trying to smoke a roll-up cigarette.*

He splutters.

VI	Mark.
	Mark.
MARK	Mm?
VI	Fancy a fuck?

Beat.

MARK   Ahmmm

Some moments.

Ahm

MARK *plays with the corner of the book, running his finger anxiously over its sharp edge.*

VI	Please.
MARK	I don't think

Silence.

VI   Please.

He comes near to her.
He sits by her.

He overcomes his revulsion.
He strokes the hub.

We could be imaginative.

MARK   (*Involuntary laugh.*)

She laughs a bit too.

Are you dead?
I don't know.

Is that you?

VI   (*Singing, Prince.*) 'Could I be?
The most beautiful hub in the world?'

MARK   (*Joining in.*) 'Plain to see
You're the reason that God made the girl'

BOTH   'Doo doo doo do doo doo.
Could I be? (uh)
The most beautiful hub in the world?'

VI   Shamon!

Pause.

MARK   You look ridiculous.

VI   You could get something.

Beat.

MARK   What?

A hat?

VI   Fuck right off.

Pause.

Tech.

He nods.

MARK   Simulator.
I could go to someone.

MARK *thinks*.

They'd know.

Unless.

VI   No.

MARK   Maybe?

VI   No, you couldn't.

MARK   Mightn't suspect an implant.

          He gestures to above his eye.

VI   But.

MARK   Not in me, anyway.

VI   You've never had anything done. Ever.

MARK   I know.

VI   No. Mister purist – Mister ultra-clean, law-abiding –

MARK   Exactly.

VI   You'd. Do that?
          Get something done?

          Would it work?

MARK   Don't know.

          Beat.

VI   What kind?

          He points to his eyes.

          I can tell you're pointing but I don't have eyes any more, Mark.

MARK   O sorry. (*Suggestion*.) Augmented reality lens? (*Wistful*.) I'd get to see you.

VI   Feel me?

MARK   Feel you.

              Pause.

VI   Forget it.
              No. You can't.
              It's okay, I'm fine like this.

MARK   Vi. You're.

              Beat.
              He kisses the hub.

              It nicks his face, the sharp bits.

              I love you.

              Rests his head on her.
              Squeezes bodily up against it.

              Sighs a soul-shattering sigh.

              *

              The flower boxes and baskets are gone. The
              cottage surfaces glitch occasionally. We can now
              identify smart surfaces in need of upgrades. The
              place has been let go, is in poor shape.

              He enters suddenly, excited.
              He checks the window, closes the blind.
              He is dressed up for the occasion, scrubbed up
              and smart again.
              He gingerly removes a dressing from his forehead.
              He has a prominent, fresh scar across it.

MARK   Okay it's installed!

              He listens.
              No answer.
              He examines the wound in the mirror. Eugh.
              Smoothes his hair.

              He arranges VI's components, carefully. Humming
              to himself.

Touches the remains lovingly. Really feels them in his hands.

Gestures. Her music plays.

Violet?

Unravels an item of her clothing. Breathes in the remains of her scent.

I've done it Violet!

Feels – mad.
If I'd ever done drugs, guess it'd feel like that.
Proud?

Quite easy to get in the end. Illegal things are kind of easy to get, aren't they? Think I'm kind of good at it. Being a – (*Criminal voice.*) *law-breaker.*
Only took an hour. In and out. Chop shop.

Proud?
I'd do it again. I'd do anything.

You. Ahm.
Sorry I never listened to you. Sorry about that.
Sorry I made you feel. You had to lie.
I love who you are.
I love you more, now you've – kicked my ass.

Violet?

Silence.

Violet?

It's not working. He deflates.

Violet?

He touches her remains.

Puts a jaunty hat on her. Admires the effect.
Not quite right.

He fetches the toaster with the face.
Pops it on top of the collection.
No, no. He hurriedly hides the toaster away again.

He sits with her.

He touches her remains against himself.
Eventually, he unzips himself.
Quickly zips himself up again.
No.
Shakes his head, laughs.

Does a circuit of the room.

Another little dance, psyching himself up.
Reapproaches the collection of objects.

He makes love, privately.

He tries to get closer to the components.

VOICE   SIMULATE?

He is suddenly hopeful.

SIMULATE?

MARK   NnnNGHYES. 'Simulate.'

Nothing happens.
He stops, exasperated.

Darkness.
Flicker. A glitch.
Her profile headshot appears. An inappropriate,
silly picture. Cheery waiting/menu music loops.

(*From the dark*.) Stupid, useless, second-rate /
lump of dirty

VOICE   SIMULATE?

MARK   YES.

The VR operates.

Suddenly: VI *is there, glitching occasionally.*

He laughs, triumphant: a hand goes to his new
implant – it works.

She waggles her limbs. Checks herself out.

They assess one another, shy, excited.

VI   Hello stranger.

MARK   (*Emotional.*) Hello, Vi.

            They come together, gentle.

            Didn't think it was going to work there.

            She touches his eyes, his ears, searchingly.

VI   Implant?

            He nods.

            She touches his scar.

            I'm in your head?

            She looks down, chuckles.

            Zip's undone.

MARK   (*Soft.*) Missed you.

            Missed you so, so, so much.

            Everything's perfect now, isn't it?

            They dance like that, blissful.

            End.

**Watford
Palace Theatre**

Watford Palace Theatre is a local theatre with a national reputation.

The creative hub at the heart of Watford, the Palace engages people through commissioning, creating and presenting high-quality theatre, and developing audiences, artists and communities through exciting opportunities to participate. Contributing to the identity of Watford and Hertfordshire, the Palace enriches people's lives, increases pride in the town, and raises the profile of the area. The beautiful 600-seat Edwardian Palace theatre is a Grade II-listed building, busy with live performances and film screenings seven days a week, offering world-class art to the tens of thousands of people visiting the theatre each year.

Recently, the Palace has enjoyed critical acclaim for its productions of Ronald Howard's *Equally Divided*, Neil Simon's *Lost in Yonkers*, Charlotte Keatley's *Our Father*, Julian Mitchell's *Family Business*, Gary Owen's *Mrs Reynolds and the Ruffian* (TMA Best New Play nomination) and Neil Simon's *Brighton Beach Memoirs* (TMA Best Supporting Performance in a Play nomination).

The Palace has co-produced a number of acclaimed new plays including *Jumpers for Goalposts* by Tom Wells, co-produced with Paines Plough and Hull Truck; *Medea* by Mike Bartlett, co-produced with Headlong and Citizens Theatre, Glasgow; *After the Rainfall* by Curious Directive; *Bunny* by Jack Thorne, a Fringe First-winning production in association with nabokov and the Mercury Colchester; and *Young Pretender* by E.V. Crowe, co-produced with nabokov and Hull Truck Theatre in association with Mercury Colchester.

Projects such as *Ballroom of Joys and Sorrows*, *Celebrate Eid*, *Diwali at the Palace*, *Celebrate Vaisakhi* and *Black History Month* have brought together the creativity of Watford's diverse communities. These build on the regular programme of Palace and Hertfordshire County Youth Theatres, adult workshops, backstage tours, community choir and extensive work with schools.

Supported by
**ARTS COUNCIL
ENGLAND**

www.nickhernbooks.co.uk

facebook.com/nickhernbooks

twitter.com/nickhernbooks